DIM SUM

Dad -
Merry Christmas 2003
lots of love,

Siân
xxx

Simple and Delicious

DIM SUM

Vicki Liley

APPLE

Introducing Dim Sum

A Cantonese specialty, dim sum (variously translated as "dot hearts," "heart warmers," and "heart's delight") is the collective name for a variety of small, delicious snacks. It includes steamed or fried dumplings with meat or seafood fillings, steamed buns, shrimp balls and always a few desserts.

It is the Chinese custom to enjoy these tiny morsels with a pot or two of Chinese tea. Dim sum, or yum cha, as it is sometimes known, has become a tradition on Sunday mornings in most cities with a sizeable Chinese population. The little delicacies are displayed on trays and trolleys which pass by your table, tempting you to try them. Some trolleys are stacked with steaming buns in bamboo steamers, others with hot fried spring rolls and other "wrapped" dishes. The trolleys are brought around constantly so you need take only one or two dishes at a time and enjoy them when they're freshly cooked.

At home, dim sum is a different story: you can't possibly make the huge selection available to you in a restaurant. Instead choose two or three different dishes—most recipes can be prepared ahead of time, leaving the steaming or frying to be done at the last minute. All you need in the way of equipment is a wok and a bamboo steamer or two. Dim sum dishes can't be left sitting around: hot dishes should be served as hot as possible, and many are accompanied by soy sauce, chili sauce or a special dipping sauce.

One or two dim sum dishes make an elegant and surprising appetizer to serve with drinks before dinner, and it is exceptional cocktail food (for a cocktail party of any size, you'll need a helper in the kitchen to keep the food coming). If you are serving a dim sum brunch, allow eight to ten bite-sized pieces per person and serve the food on small plates or in the steamers in which they are cooked. Set each place with a small bowl and chopsticks so diners can help themselves to the dishes, and serve with Chinese tea.

Equipment and Utensils

A wok is the perfect size and shape for steaming and deep-frying dim sum recipes. Carbon steel or rolled steel woks, the popular inexpensive vessels you see in Asian stores, are coated with a thin film of lacquer to prevent rusting. The film needs to be removed before the wok can be used. The best way to do this is to place the wok on the stove top, fill with cold water and add 2 tablespoons baking soda (bicarbonate of soda). Bring the mixture to the boil and boil rapidly for 15 minutes. Drain and scrub off the coating with a nylon pad. Repeat the process if any coating still remains. Then rinse and dry the wok. It is now ready to be seasoned.

Carbon steel, rolled steel and cast-iron woks require seasoning before use. This creates a smooth surface that keeps food from sticking to it and prevents it discoloring. To season a wok, place over low heat. Have paper towels and vegetable oil handy. When the wok is hot, carefully wipe it with an oiled paper towel. Repeat the process with fresh towels until they come away clean, without any trace of color.

A seasoned wok should not be scrubbed clean with detergent after cooking. Instead, use hot water and a sponge or nylon pad. Dry the wok well after washing, heat it gently, rub it over with an oiled paper towel and store in a dry, well-ventilated place. Long periods without use can cause the oil coating on the wok to become rancid. Using your wok is the best way to prevent this occurring.

There are a number of cooking utensils that go hand in hand with a wok. Bamboo steamers can be stacked on top of each other over a wok of simmering water, allowing the cook to prepare an entire meal at once or to cook one dish in several batches. They are available in many sizes at Asian supermarkets, and only need to be rinsed in hot water after cooking. Allow them to dry thoroughly before storing. Other handy utensils are a slotted spoon or wire mesh skimmer for removing deep-fried foods from hot oil; a good-quality cleaver for chopping; and extra-long cooking chopsticks for stirring and lifting food.

Ingredients

BOK CHOY Asian variety of cabbage with thick, white stalks and mild-flavored, dark green leaves. Also known as Chinese cabbage. If unavailable, use Chinese broccoli or choy sum.

CHINESE BROCCOLI Bitter-tasting broccoli with white flowers. Also known as gai laan. Chinese broccoli and choy sum can be used in place of each other.

CHINESE DRIED MUSHROOMS Intensely flavorful, dark mushrooms that need to rehydrated before use. Soak, off heat, in boiling water for 10–15 minutes and squeeze dry before using. Discard tough stems.

CHINESE SAUSAGES (LOP CHONG) Smoked pork sausages that are highly seasoned and slightly sweet. They are dry in texture and usually red in color, and are sold in the refrigerated section of Asian butchers and supermarkets. They should be steamed for 15 minutes or baked before eating.

CHOY SUM Popular and widely available Chinese green vegetable with yellow flowers and thin stalks. Every part of the mild-flavored vegetable can be used. Also known as flowering cabbage.

HOISIN SAUCE Sweet, thick Chinese sauce made from soybeans and also containing vinegar, sugar, chili peppers and other seasonings. It can be stored indefinitely in the refrigerator. Also called Chinese barbecue sauce.

RICE PAPER WRAPPERS Made from rice flour, water and salt, these brittle, paper-thin wrappers are dipped in water before being used to wrap food. They are eaten raw or can be fried, providing a crisp casing.

RICE WINE Sweet, low-alcohol Chinese wine, also known as shaoxing wine or shaoxing yellow rice wine, made from fermented glutinous rice. Sake or dry sherry can be substituted.

SHIITAKE MUSHROOMS Meaty mushrooms with light or dark brown caps. To rehydrate dried shiitakes, soak, off heat, in boiling water for 10–15 minutes and squeeze dry before slicing or chopping.

SESAME OIL / ASIAN SESAME OIL Strong-tasting oil pressed from roasted sesame seeds, mainly used as a flavoring. There is no substitute.

SPRING ROLL WRAPPERS Sheets of rice flour dough, used to enclose savory fillings. They are rolled into a cigar shape and deep-fried. Sold frozen, defrost, separate, and cover with a damp kitchen towel while preparing.

WATER CHESTNUTS Tuber of plants grown in Asia, round in shape with subtly sweet, crunchy flesh. Widely available canned; store in clean water in the refrigerator for up to 3 weeks after opening. If unavailable, use diced celery for a texture substitute.

WONTON WRAPPERS Thin sheets of wheat-based or egg-based dough, square or circular in shape, used to enclose a variety of fillings. Available fresh or frozen.

Step-by-step Guide

Basic dumplings

1. Place wonton wrapper on a work surface, spoon in filling, brush edges with water.

2. Fold in half and pinch to seal or, to create a pouch, gather edges together around the filling and twist slightly to seal. Tape the base of the dumpling on the work surface to flatten. Cover with plastic wrap while you make remaining dumplings.

Basic buns

1. Divide dough into walnut-sized rounds. Roll or press each piece out to a circle. Cover dough with a damp kitchen towel.

2. Working with one dough round at a time, spoon filling into the center. Gather edges together and twist to seal dough. Cut out squares of parchment (baking paper) and place buns, sealed side down, onto paper.

Deep-frying

1. Pour oil into a large wok and heat until it reaches 375°F (190°C). To test heat, drop a small bread cube into the oil – it should sizzle and turn golden.

2. Working in batches, add food and fry until golden. Use a wire mesh skimmer or slotted spoon to remove the food from the oil and drain on paper towels.

Steaming

1. Line a medium bamboo steamer with parchment (baking paper), or cut individual pieces of parchment for dumplings and buns. Arrange food in steamer and cover with lid.

2. Half fill a medium wok with water (steamer should not touch water) and bring to the boil.

3. Place the steamer in the wok and steam for the required time, adding more boiling water to the wok when necessary. Lift the steamer off the wok and carefully remove the food.

NOTE Bamboo steamers can be stacked on top of one another to cook several different dishes at the same time, or to cook one dish in batches.

Dim Sum Classics

Stuffed crab claws

Makes 12

12 cooked crab claws
1 lb (500 g) jumbo shrimp (green king prawns), peeled and deveined
2 cloves garlic
3 teaspoons peeled and grated fresh ginger
1 egg white
2 teaspoons fish sauce
¼ teaspoon salt
4 scallions (shallots/spring onions), roughly chopped
¼ cup (1½ oz/45 g) finely chopped celery
3 cups (24 fl oz/750 ml) vegetable oil for deep-frying
¼ cup (1 oz/30 g) cornstarch (cornflour)
BATTER
½ cup (2 oz/60 g) cornstarch (cornflour)
½ cup (2 oz/60 g) all-purpose (plain) flour
½ teaspoon baking powder
½ teaspoon salt
1 cup (8 fl oz/250 ml) water

Gently remove the crab shell, leaving shell on nipper end to make a handle for holding crab claws. Place shrimp, garlic, ginger, egg white, fish sauce and salt in a food processor and process until smooth. Transfer to a bowl. Stir in scallions and celery.

Divide mixture into 12 portions. With wet hands, flatten each portion in palm of hand. Place flesh end of crab claw into center of shrimp mixture. Wrap shrimp around crab flesh. Wet hands again and mold shrimp evenly all over crab flesh.

For batter, sift dry ingredients into a mixing bowl. Gradually add water and mix to a smooth batter.

Heat oil in a large wok to 375°F (190°C), or until a small bread cube dropped in oil sizzles and turns golden. Dip crab claws in cornstarch, shaking off any excess. Working in batches, holding nipper end of claw, dip into batter, then fry until golden, 2–3 minutes. Remove with a slotted spoon and drain on paper towels. Serve hot with Chili Sauce or Lime and Fish Sauce.

Golden shrimp balls

Makes 12

12 slices stale white bread
16 oz (500 g) jumbo shrimp (green king prawns), peeled and deveined
6 canned water chestnuts, drained and finely chopped
2 oz (60 g) bacon, rind removed and finely chopped
1 teaspoon sugar
½ teaspoon salt
2 teaspoons cornstarch (cornflour)
3 cups (24 fl oz/750 ml) vegetable oil for deep-frying

Remove crusts from bread. Cut bread into ¼-inch (6-mm) cubes. Spread out on a tray and allow to dry at room temperature. Flatten shrimp with the back of a cleaver, then finely chop. Combine shrimp, water chestnuts and bacon in a bowl and stir in sugar, salt and cornstarch. Mix well. Cover and chill for 30 minutes.

Roll 1 tablespoon of shrimp mixture in bread cubes to coat. Repeat with remaining mixture. Heat oil in a large wok or saucepan until it reaches 375°F (190°C) on a deep-frying thermometer, or until a small bread cube dropped in oil sizzles and turns golden. Working in batches, add shrimp balls and fry until golden, 1–2 minutes. Using a slotted spoon, remove from oil and drain on paper towels. Serve hot with Quick Sweet-and-Sour Sauce.

Flower dumplings

Makes 24

24 wonton wrappers

1 lb (500 g) ground (minced) chicken

6 canned water chestnuts, drained and
finely chopped

1 small carrot, finely chopped

2 scallions (shallots/spring onions),
finely chopped

1 teaspoon peeled and grated
fresh ginger

1 teaspoon Asian sesame oil

1 teaspoon rice wine

1 teaspoon soy sauce

1 teaspoon salt

2 teaspoons sugar

2 tablespoons cornstarch (cornflour)

In a bowl, combine chicken, water chestnuts, carrot, scallions, ginger, sesame oil, rice wine, soy sauce, salt, sugar and cornstarch. Using wet hands, mix until well combined.

Place wonton wrappers on work surface and cover with a damp kitchen towel. Working with one wrapper at a time, place 3 teaspoons of chicken filling in the center. Gather edges around filling, forming a basket, and gently squeeze center

of dumpling to expose the filling at the top. Tap bottom of dumpling on work surface to flatten. Cover with plastic wrap and set aside. Repeat with remaining wrappers.

Line a medium bamboo steamer with parchment (baking paper). Half fill a medium wok with water (steamer should not touch water) and bring to a boil. Arrange dumplings in steamer, cover, and place steamer over boiling water. Steam for 12 minutes, adding more boiling water to wok when necessary. Lift steamer off wok and carefully remove dumplings. Serve warm with soy sauce or Ginger Soy Dipping Sauce.

Traditional mini spring rolls

Makes 20

2 tablespoons vegetable oil
2 cloves garlic, finely chopped
2 teaspoons peeled and grated
   fresh ginger
3½ oz (100 g) ground (minced) pork
3½ oz (100 g) ground (minced) chicken
2 oz (60 g) ground (minced) shrimp
   (prawns)
6 canned water chestnuts, drained and
   finely chopped
4 scallions (shallots/spring onions),
   finely chopped
2 stalks celery, finely chopped

1 small carrot, finely chopped
1 cup (3 oz/90 g) shredded Chinese
   cabbage
2 teaspoons cornstarch (cornflour)
2 tablespoon oyster sauce
1 tablespoon soy sauce
2 tablespoons chicken stock
1 teaspoon Asian sesame oil
20 frozen mini spring roll wrappers, about
   4½ inches (11.5 cm) square, thawed
2 teaspoons cornstarch (cornflour)
   mixed with 2 tablespoons water
4 cups (32 fl oz/1 L) vegetable oil for
   deep-frying

Heat 1 tablespoon oil in a wok over medium heat. Add garlic and ginger, and cook until aromatic, about 1 minute. Stir in pork, chicken and shrimp; cook, stirring, until mixture changes color, about 3 minutes. Remove from heat, transfer to a bowl. Using same wok, heat remaining 1 tablespoon oil over medium heat. Add water chestnuts, scallions, celery, carrot and cabbage. Raise heat to high and stir-fry until softened, about 2 minutes. In a small bowl, combine cornstarch, oyster sauce, soy sauce and stock. Add to wok, bring to a boil, reduce heat to medium and cook until sauce thickens, 1–2 minutes. Remove from heat; allow to cool. Stir in pork mixture and sesame oil, mix well.

Separate spring roll wrappers, and cover with a damp kitchen towel. Working with one wrapper at a time, wet edges with cornstarch and water mixture. Place 1 tablespoon of filling in center of wrapper and roll up diagonally, tucking in edges. Seal edges with cornstarch mixture. Repeat with remaining wrappers.

Heat oil in a large wok to 375°F (190°C), or until a small bread cube dropped in oil sizzles and turns golden. Working in batches, add rolls and fry until golden, about 1 minute. Using a slotted spoon, remove from oil and drain on paper towels. Serve with Quick Sweet-and-Sour Sauce.

Pearl balls

Makes about 20
1 cup (7 oz/220 g) short-grain
  white rice
1 lb (500 g) ground (minced) pork
4 scallions (shallots/spring onions),
  chopped
4 canned water chestnuts, drained
  and chopped

1 teaspoon sugar
1 teaspoon salt
2 cloves garlic, crushed
2 teaspoons peeled and grated
  fresh ginger
1 teaspoon Asian sesame oil
2 teaspoons light soy sauce
2 teaspoons rice wine

Place rice in a medium bowl. Cover with cold water and let stand for 30 minutes. Drain, spread out onto a paper towel–lined tray and allow to dry.

In a bowl, combine pork, scallions, water chestnuts, sugar, salt, garlic, ginger, sesame oil, soy sauce and rice wine. Using wet hands, mix until well combined. Divide mixture into 20 portions.

Line a bamboo steamer with banana leaves or parchment (baking paper).

Using wet hands, shape pork mixture into small balls. Roll each ball in rice until well coated.

Half fill a medium wok with water (steamer should not touch water) and bring to a boil. Working in batches, arrange balls in prepared steamer, allowing room for rice to expand.

Cover and place steamer over boiling water. Steam for 30 minutes, adding more boiling water to wok when necessary. Lift steamer off wok and carefully remove balls. Serve warm with soy sauce or Ginger Soy Dipping Sauce.

Shrimp toasts

This Western-adapted recipe is a favorite in most dim sum tea houses.

Makes 14

4 slices stale white bread

1 lb (500g) jumbo shrimp (green king prawns), peeled and deveined

2 cloves garlic

2 teaspoons peeled and grated fresh ginger

1 teaspoon sugar

½ teaspoon salt

1 tablespoon cornstarch (cornflour)

1 egg white

1 teaspoon Asian sesame oil

4 scallions (shallots/spring onions), finely chopped

1 egg, beaten

1 cup (4 oz/125 g) dry breadcrumbs

3 cups (24 fl oz/750 ml) vegetable oil for deep-frying

Remove crusts from bread and cut each slice into 4 triangles. Allow bread to dry out at room temperature. Place shrimp, garlic, ginger, sugar, salt, cornstarch, egg white and sesame oil in a food processor and process until smooth. Transfer to a bowl, then stir in scallions.

Place 1 tablespoon of shrimp filling in the center of each bread triangle. Brush shrimp filling and bread edges with beaten egg and sprinkle with breadcrumbs. Pat shrimp mixture into a pyramid shape, shaking off any excess crumbs.

Heat oil in a large wok until it reaches 375°F (190°C) on a deep-frying thermometer, or until a small bread cube dropped in oil sizzles and turns golden. Working in batches, fry toasts until golden on both sides, 1–2 minutes. Using a slotted spoon, remove from oil and drain on paper towels. Serve hot with Sweet Cilantro Sauce or Quick Sweet-and-Sour Sauce.

Dumplings

Shanghai dumplings

Sometimes known as Shanghai street dumplings and originally made in the 1950s on the streets of Hong Kong on coal stoves by Shanghai refugees, these dumplings are still a favorite.

Makes 16

1 lb (500 g) bok choy
1 lb (500 g) ground (minced) pork
1 tablespoon peeled and grated
   fresh ginger
¼ teaspoon salt

1 teaspoon Asian sesame oil
1 teaspoon white vinegar
1 tablespoon oyster sauce
16 wonton wrappers
4 tablespoons vegetable oil
⅔ cup (5 fl oz/150 ml) water

Cook bok choy in a pan of boiling water for 2 minutes, then drain and refresh in cold water. Finely chop bok choy. In a bowl, combine bok choy, pork, ginger, salt, sesame oil, vinegar and oyster sauce. Using wet hands, mix well.

Place wonton wrappers on work surface and cover with a damp kitchen towel. Working with one wrapper at a time, lay wrapper on work surface and place 3 teaspoons of pork filling in the center. Brush edges with water. Gather edges together and twist to seal. Place on a plate, sealed side down, cover with plastic wrap and set aside. Repeat with remaining wonton wrappers.

Heat 2 tablespoons oil in a wok or frying pan over medium heat. Working in batches, cook 8 dumplings, sealed side down, until golden, about 3 minutes. Carefully add half the water (liquid will sizzle and spatter a little; be careful) and cook until water evaporates. Reduce heat to low and continue to cook until dumplings are translucent, 3–4 minutes. Remove from pan. Repeat with remaining dumplings and remaining oil and water. Serve warm with soy sauce or Easy Plum Sauce.

Cook-and-sell dumplings

These dumplings were traditionally cooked and sold on the streets, hence their name.

Makes 12

12 wonton wrappers

6 Chinese dried mushrooms

4 oz (125 g) jumbo shrimp (green king prawns), peeled, deveined and finely chopped

8 oz (250 g) ground (minced) pork

4 scallions (shallots/spring onions), finely chopped

½ teaspoon salt

1 teaspoon sugar

1 tablespoon oyster sauce

1 teaspoon Asian sesame oil

1 tablespoon cornstarch (cornflour)

Place mushrooms in a small bowl, add boiling water to cover and let stand until softened, 10–15 minutes. Drain and squeeze excess liquid from mushrooms. Finely chop; discard thick stems. Place mushrooms, shrimp, pork, scallions, salt, sugar, oyster sauce, sesame oil and cornstarch in a bowl. Using wet hands, mix well.

Cover wonton wrappers with a damp kitchen towel. Working with one wrapper at a time, lay wrapper on work surface and place 2 teaspoons of filling in the center. Gather edges around filling, forming a basket, and gently squeeze center of dumpling to expose the filling at the top. Tap bottom of dumpling on work surface to flatten, cover with plastic wrap and set aside. Repeat with rest of wrappers.

Line a medium bamboo steamer with parchment (baking paper). Half fill a medium wok with water (steamer should not touch water) and bring to a boil. Arrange wontons in steamer, cover and place steamer over boiling water. Steam for 10 minutes, adding more boiling water to wok if necessary. Lift steamer off wok and remove dumplings. Serve warm with soy sauce or Ginger Soy Dipping Sauce.

Salmon money bags

This recipe is a tasty Western adaptation of the traditional favorite.

Makes 12

12 wonton wrappers

9 oz (280 g) Atlantic salmon, bones and
   skin removed, finely chopped

3 tablespoons cream cheese

3 scallions (shallots/spring onions),
   finely chopped

2 teaspoons peeled and grated
   fresh ginger

¼ teaspoon salt

pinch five-spice powder

1 teaspoon grated lime zest

1 egg yolk

12 chives

In a bowl, combine salmon, cream cheese, scallions, ginger, salt, five-spice
powder, lime zest and egg yolk. Using wet hands, mix well.

Place wonton wrappers on work surface and cover with a damp kitchen towel.
Working with one wrapper at a time, lay wrapper on work surface and place
2 teaspoons of filling in the center. Brush edges of wrapper with water. Gather
edges together and twist to seal. Cover with a damp kitchen towel and set aside.

Repeat with remaining wonton
wrappers.

Line a medium bamboo steamer
with parchment (baking paper). Half
fill a medium wok with water (steamer
should not touch water) and bring to
a boil. Arrange filled wontons in
steamer, cover and place steamer over
boiling water. Steam for 8 minutes,
adding more boiling water to wok
when necessary. Lift steamer off wok
and carefully remove dumplings. Dip
chives into bowl of hot water and tie
one loosely around the top of each
money bag. Serve warm with soy
sauce or Thai sweet chili sauce.

Cockscomb dumplings

These dumplings are so named because they resemble the crest of a rooster.

Makes 16
8 oz (250 g) ground (minced) chicken
4 scallions (shallots/spring onions),
   finely chopped
1 teaspoon peeled and grated fresh
   ginger
3 canned water chestnuts, drained and
   finely chopped
2 tablespoons finely chopped, drained
   canned bamboo shoots

2 teaspoons rice wine
2 teaspoons salt
1 teaspoon sugar
1 teaspoon soy sauce
1 teaspoon Asian sesame oil
1 tablespoon oyster sauce
1½ tablespoons cornstarch (cornflour)
16 round wonton wrappers
6 cups (48 fl oz/1.5 L) water
1 tablespoon vegetable oil

In a bowl, combine ground chicken, scallions, ginger, water chestnuts, bamboo shoots, rice wine, 1 teaspoon salt, sugar, soy sauce, sesame oil, oyster sauce and cornstarch. Using wet hands, mix until well combined.

Place wonton wrappers on work surface and cover with a damp kitchen towel. Working with one wrapper at a time, place wrapper in a gow gee press and put 2 teaspoons of filling in the center. Brush edges of wrapper with water. Close gow gee press firmly to seal edges together. Alternatively, place wrapper on work surface, spoon in filling, brush with water and fold in half to form a semicircle. Pinch edges together to make a frill. Cover with a damp kitchen towel and repeat with remaining wrappers.

Pour water into a medium wok or saucepan, add remaining 1 teaspoon salt and vegetable oil, and bring to a boil. Working in batches, cook dumplings in boiling water for 5 minutes. Remove from pan with a slotted spoon. Run cold water over cooked dumplings. Serve immediately with Lime and Cilantro Dipping Sauce.

Pork swallows

Once fried, these tasty morsels resemble flying swallows.

Makes 20
20 square wonton wrappers
8 oz (250 g) ground (minced) pork
4 oz (125 g) jumbo shrimp (green
king prawns), peeled, deveined
and finely chopped
1 tablespoon peeled and grated
fresh ginger

4 scallions (shallots/spring onions),
finely chopped
2 teaspoons rice wine
½ teaspoon salt
1 teaspoon Asian sesame oil
3 teaspoons cornstarch (cornflour)
4 cups (32 fl oz/1 L) vegetable oil
for deep-frying

Place ground pork, shrimp and ginger in a food processor and process until smooth. Transfer to a bowl. Add scallions, rice wine, salt, sesame oil and cornstarch. Using wet hands, mix until well combined.

Place wonton wrappers on work surface and cover with a damp kitchen towel. Working with one wrapper at a time, place 2 teaspoons of filling in the center and brush edges of wrapper with water. Fold wonton corners into the center, forming an envelope shape. Using your fingertips, press along diagonal edges to seal. Cover with a damp kitchen towel and repeat with remaining wrappers.

Heat oil in a large wok until it reaches 375°F (190°C) on a deep-frying thermometer, or until a small bread cube dropped in oil sizzles and turns golden. Working in batches, add wontons and fry until golden on both sides, 2–3 minutes. Using a slotted spoon, remove from oil and drain on paper towels. Serve hot with soy sauce or Lime and Cilantro Dipping Sauce.

Wok-fried money bags

Money bags are shaped into little pouches gathered at the top, reminiscent of the little leather sacs used to carry money in China.

Makes 20
20 wonton wrappers
1 bunch bok choy, washed and
  leaves separated
8 oz (250 g) ground (minced) chicken
1 teaspoon Asian sesame oil
3 scallions (shallots/spring onions),
  finely chopped

1 teaspoon peeled and grated
  fresh ginger
1 clove garlic, finely chopped
1 teaspoon rice wine
2 teaspoons oyster sauce
1 teaspoon soy sauce
pinch salt
3 teaspoons cornstarch (cornflour)

Cook bok choy in a pan of boiling water for 2 minutes. Drain, refresh in cold water and chop finely. In a bowl, combine bok choy, ground chicken, sesame oil, scallions, ginger, garlic, rice wine, oyster sauce, soy sauce, salt and cornstarch. Using wet hands, mix until well combined.

Place wonton wrappers on work surface and cover with a damp kitchen towel. Working with one wrapper at a time, place 2 teaspoons of filling in the center and brush edges of wrapper with water. Gather edges together and twist to seal.

Cover with a damp kitchen towel and set aside. Repeat with remaining wrappers.

Heat oil in a large wok until it reaches 375°F (190°C) on a deep-frying thermometer, or until a small bread cube dropped in oil sizzles and turns golden. Working in batches, add wontons and fry until golden, 1–2 minutes. Using a slotted spoon, remove from oil and drain on paper towels. Serve hot with soy, hoisin or plum sauce.

Crisp-fried gow gee

Makes 16

6 Chinese dried mushrooms
4 oz (125 g) jumbo shrimp (green king prawns), peeled, deveined and finely chopped
8 oz (250 g) ground (minced) pork
½ cup (4 oz/125 g) finely chopped, drained canned bamboo shoots
6 scallions (shallots/spring onions), finely chopped
1 clove garlic, finely chopped
2 teaspoons Asian sesame oil
3 teaspoons soy sauce
2 teaspoons rice wine
20 round wonton wrappers
4 cups (32 fl oz/1 L) vegetable oil for deep-frying

Place mushrooms in a small bowl, add boiling water to cover and let stand until softened, 10–15 minutes. Drain and squeeze excess liquid from mushrooms. Finely chop, discarding thick stems. In a bowl, combine mushrooms, shrimp, ground pork, bamboo shoots, scallions, garlic, sesame oil, soy sauce and rice wine. Using wet hands, mix until well combined.

Place wonton wrappers on work surface and cover with a damp kitchen towel. Working with one wrapper at a time, place in a gow gee press and put 2 teaspoons of filling in the center. Brush edges of wrapper with water. Close gow gee press firmly to seal edges together. Alternatively, place wrapper on work surface, spoon in filling, brush with water and fold in half to form a semicircle. Pinch edges together to make a frill. Cover with a damp kitchen towel and repeat with remaining wrappers.

Heat oil in a large wok until it reaches 375°F (190°C) on a deep-frying thermometer, or until a small bread cube dropped in oil sizzles and turns golden. Working in batches, add gow gee and fry until golden on both sides, 1–2 minutes. Using a slotted spoon, remove from oil and drain on paper towels. Serve hot with soy sauce or Chili Sauce.

Steamed spinach and ginger dumplings

Makes 15

1 tablespoon vegetable oil

1 tablespoon peeled and grated fresh ginger

3 cloves garlic, crushed

2 bunches spinach, washed and finely chopped

½ teaspoon salt

15 wonton wrappers

Heat oil in a wok or frying pan over medium heat. Add ginger and garlic, and stir-fry until aromatic, about 1 minute. Add spinach and stir-fry until soft, 2–3 minutes. Remove from heat and add salt. Transfer mixture to bowl and allow to cool completely.

Place wonton wrappers on work surface and cover with a damp kitchen towel. Working with one wrapper at a time, place 2 teaspoons of filling in the center and brush edges of wrapper with water. Gather edges together and twist to seal. Cover with a damp kitchen towel and set aside. Repeat with remaining wrappers.

Line a medium bamboo steamer with parchment (baking paper). Half fill a medium wok with water (steamer should not touch water) and bring to a boil. Arrange dumplings in steamer, cover and place steamer over boiling water. Steam for 10 minutes, adding more boiling water to wok when necessary. Lift steamer off wok and carefully remove dumplings. Serve warm with soy sauce.

Snowpea shoot dumplings

Makes 15

4 oz (125 g) fresh snowpea (mange-
tout) shoots, roughly chopped

4 oz (125 g) jumbo shrimp (green king
prawns), peeled, deveined and
coarsely chopped

2 teaspoons peeled and grated fresh
ginger

3 teaspoons oyster sauce

1 teaspoon soy sauce

1 teaspoon rice wine

¼ teaspoon salt

½ teaspoon sugar

1 teaspoon Asian sesame oil

1 tablespoon cornstarch (cornflour)

15 round wonton wrappers

Blanch snowpea shoots in a pan of boiling water for 1 minute. Drain and refresh immediately in cold water. In a bowl, combine snowpea shoots, shrimp, ginger, oyster sauce, soy sauce, rice wine, salt, sugar, sesame oil and cornstarch. Using wet hands, mix until well combined.

Place wonton wrappers on work surface and cover with a damp kitchen towel. Working with one wrapper at a time, place 3 teaspoons of filling in the center and brush edges of wrapper with water. Fold three sides of wrapper into the center, forming a triangular shape. Using your fingertips, press edges of wrapper together. Cover with a damp kitchen towel and set aside. Repeat with remaining wonton wrappers.

Line a medium bamboo steamer with parchment (baking paper). Half fill a medium wok with water (steamer should not touch water) and bring to a boil. Arrange dumplings in steamer, cover and place steamer over boiling water. Steam for 10 minutes, adding more boiling water to wok when necessary. Lift steamer off wok and carefully remove dumplings. Serve warm with soy sauce.

Buns

Red bean paste buns

Makes 8

1¼ cups (10 oz/300 g) all-purpose (plain) flour
1½ teaspoons baking powder
¼ cup (1¾ oz/50 g) superfine (caster) sugar
¼ cup (2 fl oz/60 ml) milk
2 tablespoons water
1½ tablespoons vegetable oil
¾ cup (7½ oz/235 g) canned red bean paste
2 teaspoons black sesame seeds

To make dough, sift flour and baking powder into a bowl and add sugar. Gradually add combined milk, water and oil, mixing to form a soft dough. Turn out onto a floured work surface and knead until smooth, 1–2 minutes. Wrap dough in plastic wrap and chill for 1 hour.

Roll dough into a sausage shape 8 inches (20 cm) long. Cut into 8 1-inch (2.5-cm) pieces and roll each into a ball. Cover with a damp kitchen towel. Working with one piece of dough at a time, press into a cup shape. Place 1 tablespoon of red bean paste in the center of dough. Gather edges together, twist and seal. Cover with a damp kitchen towel and repeat with remaining dough.

Cut out 8 squares of parchment (baking paper) and place buns, sealed side down, on paper. Brush tops of buns with water and sprinkle with black sesame seeds. Half fill a medium wok with water (steamer should not touch water) and bring to a boil. Working in batches, arrange buns in steamer, cover and place steamer over boiling water. Steam for 20 minutes, adding more boiling water to wok when necessary.

Lift steamer off wok and carefully remove buns. Serve warm.

Lotus nut buns

Makes 16

1½ teaspoons active dry yeast

½ cup (4 fl oz/125 ml) warm water

¼ cup (1¾ oz/50 g) superfine
  (caster) sugar

1 cup (4 oz/125 g) all-purpose
  (plain) flour

½ cup (2 oz/60 g) self-rising flour

3 teaspoons butter, melted

¾ cup (7½ oz/235 g) canned lotus
  nut paste

In a small bowl, combine yeast with 2 tablespoons warm water, 1 teaspoon
sugar and 1 teaspoon all-purpose flour. Mix until well combined. Cover with a
kitchen towel and let stand in a warm place until frothy, about 15 minutes. Sift
remaining all-purpose flour and self-rising flour into a large bowl. Add remaining
sugar, yeast mixture, remaining warm water and melted butter. Mix with a
wooden spoon, to form a soft dough. Turn onto a floured work surface and knead
until smooth and elastic, 3–5 minutes. Place dough in a large oiled bowl, cover;
stand in a warm place until doubled in bulk, about 1 hour.

Punch down dough. Turn out onto a floured work surface and knead until
smooth, about 5 minutes. Divide into 16 pieces and roll or press out each piece
to form a 2¼-inch (6-cm) circle. Cover dough with a damp kitchen towel.
Working with one round of dough at a time, spoon 2 teaspoons of lotus nut paste
into the center. Gather edges together, twist to seal and cover with a kitchen

towel. Repeat with remaining dough.

Cut out 16 squares of parchment
(baking paper) and place buns, sealed
side down, on paper. Half fill medium
wok with water (steamer should not
touch water); bring to a boil. Working
in batches, arrange buns in steamer,
cover and place steamer over boiling
water. Steam 15–20 minutes, adding
more boiling water to wok when
necessary. Lift steamer off wok and
carefully remove buns. Serve warm.

Chinese pork sausage buns

Makes 12

1 cup (4 oz/125 g) self-rising flour

2 teaspoons baking powder

2 teaspoons superfine (caster) sugar

2 teaspoons lard

6 Chinese pork sausages

¼–⅓ cup (2–3 fl oz/60–90 ml)
  warm milk

1 tablespoon hoisin sauce,
  plus extra for dipping

2 teaspoons soy sauce

Sift flour and baking powder into a bowl and add sugar. Rub lard into dry ingredients using your fingertips. Gradually add enough milk to make a soft dough. Turn dough out onto a floured work surface and knead for 1–2 minutes, until smooth. Wrap in plastic wrap and let stand for 30 minutes. Meanwhile, cut sausages in half crosswise. Place in a bowl with 1 tablespoon hoisin sauce and soy sauce, mix until well coated, cover, and let stand for 25 minutes.

Turn dough out onto a floured work surface and knead for 1 minute. Roll into a thick snake shape 12 inches (30 cm) long, and cut it into 12 pieces. Cover dough with a damp kitchen towel. Working with one piece of dough at a time, rub it between floured hands to form a thin snake about 4 inches (10 cm) long. Wrap dough around sausage in a spiral pattern, leaving ends of sausage exposed, and place on an oiled tray. Repeat with remaining dough and sausages.

Line a bamboo steamer with parchment (baking paper). Half fill a medium wok with water (steamer should not touch water) and bring to a boil. Working in batches, arrange buns in prepared steamer, allowing room for buns to spread. Cover and place steamer over boiling water. Steam for 15 minutes, adding more boiling water to wok when necessary. Lift steamer off wok and carefully remove buns. Serve warm with hoisin sauce.

Steamed chicken buns

Makes 16

2½ cups (10 oz/300 g) all-purpose (plain) flour
3 teaspoons baking powder
½ cup (3¾ oz/110 g) superfine (caster) sugar
½ cup (4 fl oz/125 ml) milk
⅓ cup (3 fl oz/90 ml) water
¼ cup (2 fl oz/60 ml) vegetable oil plus1 tablespoon extra
6 Chinese dried mushrooms
3 teaspoons peeled and grated fresh ginger
8 oz (250 g) ground (minced) chicken
2 tablespoons chopped, drained canned bamboo shoots
4 scallions (shallots/spring onions), chopped
1 tablespoon oyster sauce
1 teaspoon soy sauce
1 teaspoon Asian sesame oil
¼ teaspoon salt
2 teaspoons cornstarch (cornflour) mixed with 2 tablespoons chicken stock

Sift flour and baking powder into a bowl, add sugar. Gradually add combined milk, water and ¼ cup (2 fl oz/60 ml) oil, mixing to form a soft dough. Turn out onto a floured work surface and knead until smooth, 1–2 minutes. Wrap dough in plastic wrap and chill for 1 hour.

Place mushrooms in a small bowl, add boiling water to cover and stand until softened, 10–15 minutes. Drain, squeeze liquid from mushrooms and finely chop, discarding thick stems. Heat 1 tablespoon oil in a wok over medium heat and fry ginger until aromatic, about 1 minute. Add chicken and cook until meat changes color, about 3 minutes. Stir in bamboo shoots, scallions, oyster sauce, soy sauce, sesame oil, salt and cornstarch mixture. Bring to boil; stir until sauce thickens. Remove from heat, transfer to a plate, cool.

Roll dough into a sausage shape 16 inches (40.5 cm) long. Cut into 16 1-inch (2.5-cm) pieces, and roll each into a ball. Cover with damp kitchen towel. Working with one piece at a time, press into a cup shape. Place

1 tablespoon of filling in center. Gather edges, twist and seal. Cover with a damp kitchen towel. Repeat with rest of dough.

Cut out 16 squares of parchment (baking paper) and place buns, sealed side down, on paper. Half fill medium wok with water (steamer should not touch water) and bring to boil. Working in batches, arrange buns in steamer, cover and place steamer over boiling water. Steam for 20 minutes, adding more boiling water to wok when necessary. Lift steamer off wok and remove buns. Serve with Sweet Cilantro Sauce.

Pancakes and Wraps

Peking duck pancakes

Makes 15

PANCAKES
¾ cup (3 oz/90 g) all-purpose (plain) flour
⅓ cup (1½ oz/45 g) cornstarch (cornflour)
2 eggs
¾ cup (6 fl oz/180 ml) water
¼ cup (2 fl oz/60 ml) milk
2 teaspoons superfine (caster) sugar
1 tablespoon vegetable oil

FILLING
15 scallions (shallots/spring onions)
2 carrots, peeled and cut into thin sticks
1 Chinese roast duck
¼ cup (2 fl oz/60 ml) hoisin sauce
1 tablespoon rice wine
FOR SERVING
12 chives
⅓ cup (3 fl oz/90 ml) hoisin sauce for dipping

To make pancakes, sift flour and cornstarch into a bowl. In a separate bowl, whisk together eggs, water, milk and sugar. Make a well in center of dry ingredients, gradually add egg mixture and beat until smooth.

Heat oil in a frying pan over medium heat, pour in 2 tablespoons of pancake batter and swirl pan gently to form a round pancake. Cook until golden, about 2 minutes. Turn and cook other side for 10 seconds. Remove from pan and repeat with remaining batter and oil.

To make filling, cut into each end of scallions with a sharp knife or scissors to form a fringe. Place scallions and carrots in a bowl of iced water and refrigerate for 15 minutes, or until scallions curl. Remove meat and skin from duck and roughly chop. Combine hoisin sauce and rice wine.

Lay pancakes on work surface and place 1 tablespoon of duck meat and skin in center of each one. Top with 1 teaspoon of hoisin and rice wine mixture. Add a scallion curl and 3–4 carrots sticks. Roll and secure with a chive, trimming off any excess chive. Serve with hoisin sauce as a dipping sauce.

Crispy wrapped shrimp

Makes 20
20 jumbo shrimp (green king prawns), peeled and deveined, tails intact
2 cloves garlic, finely chopped
2 tablespoons vegetable oil
20 wonton wrappers
1 egg, beaten
20 chives
3 cups (24 fl oz/750 ml) vegetable oil for deep-frying

Place shrimp in a bowl, pour in combined garlic and oil, and toss until well coated. Cover and refrigerate for 2 hours. Place wrappers on work surface and cover with a damp kitchen towel. Working with one wrapper at a time, brush edges of wrapper with beaten egg. Place a shrimp diagonally across the center and fold wrapper around shrimp.

Place chives in a bowl of hot water for 1 minute, then drain. Secure wrapper around shrimp with a chive, trimming off excess chive. Cover with a damp kitchen towel and set aside. Repeat with remaining wrappers.

Heat oil in a large wok until it reaches 375°F (190°C) on a deep-frying thermometer, or until a small bread cube dropped in oil sizzles and turns golden. Working in batches, add wrapped shrimp and fry until golden, 1–2 minutes. Using a slotted spoon, remove from oil and drain on paper towels. Serve hot with soy, hoisin or plum sauce.

Paper-wrapped shrimp rolls

Makes 20

1½ lb (750 g) jumbo shrimp (green king prawns), peeled, deveined and finely chopped
3 teaspoons peeled and grated fresh ginger
2 cloves garlic, finely chopped
4 scallions (shallots/spring onions), finely chopped
1 tablespoon cornstarch (cornflour)
20 rice paper wrappers, about 8 inches (20 cm) square (if unavailable, use spring roll wrappers or pancakes; see Peking Duck Pancakes, page 40)
2 tablespoons cornstarch (cornflour) mixed with 1½ tablespoons water
¼ cup (2 fl oz/60 ml) vegetable oil for deep-frying

In a bowl, combine shrimp, ginger, garlic, scallions and cornstarch. Using wet hands, mix until well combined. Working with one wrapper at a time, plunge it into a shallow bowl of warm water until softened, 1–2 minutes. Lay it on work surface and place 1½ tablespoons of shrimp filling in center. Brush edges of

wrapper with combined cornstarch mixture. Fold wrapper over filling, tucking in edges, and roll up to form a neat parcel. Cover with a damp kitchen towel and set aside. Repeat with remaining ingredients.

Heat oil in a wok or frying pan, until it reaches 375°F (190°C) on a deep-frying thermometer, or until a small bread cube dropped in oil sizzles and turns golden. Working in batches, add parcels and fry until golden on both sides, about 2 minutes. Shake pan from time to time to prevent parcels sticking. Remove from oil and drain on paper towels. Serve hot with hoisin sauce.

Lotus leaf wraps

Makes 10

5 dried lotus leaves, cut in half (or use banana leaves or aluminium foil)

1⅓ cups (9 oz/280 g) short-grain rice, washed and drained

4 Chinese dried mushrooms

1 tablespoon vegetable oil

2 teaspoons peeled and grated fresh ginger

6½ oz (200 g) ground (minced) chicken

4 oz (125 g) jumbo shrimp (green king prawns), peeled, deveined and finely chopped

2 Chinese pork sausages, finely chopped

1 tablespoon soy sauce

1 tablespoon rice wine

1 tablespoon oyster sauce

2 teaspoons cornstarch (cornflour) mixed with 1 tablespoon water

Soak lotus leaves in hot water until softened, about 15 minutes. Drain. Line bamboo steamer with parchment (baking paper), spread drained rice over it and cover steamer. Half fill a medium wok with water (steamer should not touch water) and bring to boil. Place steamer over boiling water and steam until rice is tender, 25–30 minutes, adding more boiling water to wok when necessary. Remove steamer, allow rice to cool, then divide into 10 portions.

Place mushrooms in a small bowl, add boiling water to cover. let stand until softened, 10–15 minutes. Drain and squeeze out excess liquid. Finely chop and discard thick stems.

Heat oil in wok over medium heat. Fry ginger until aromatic, about 30 seconds. Add chicken and shrimp, and stir-fry until mixture changes color, about 3 minutes. Add sausages, mushrooms, soy sauce, rice wine and oyster sauce and cook for 1 minute. Stir in cornstarch mixture, bring to a boil and stir until sauce thickens, about 2 minutes. Remove from heat and cool.

Place lotus leaves on work surface. Spoon a portion of rice into the center of each leaf. Place 3 teaspoons of chicken mixture over rice and mold rice around it. Fold leaf over rice to form parcel, secure with raffia or twine.

Half fill a large wok with water (steamer should not touch water) and bring to a boil. Working in batches, arrange parcels in steamer, cover and place steamer over boiling water. Steam for 15 minutes, adding more boiling water to wok when necessary. Lift steamer off wok and carefully remove parcels. Cut open to serve.

Seafood, Pork and Vegetables

Steamed scallops in shells

Makes 4 small serves
24 scallops in their shells
2 tablespoons vegetable oil
4 cloves garlic, finely chopped
6 scallions (shallots/spring onions), chopped
GINGER AND SCALLION SAUCE
6 scallions (shallots/spring onions), cut into shreds
3 tablespoons vegetable oil
2-inch (5-cm) piece fresh ginger, cut into fine shreds
1 green chili pepper, seeded and sliced
4 tablespoons soy sauce
2 tablespoons water

Clean scallops and return to shells. Heat oil in a small saucepan over medium heat and fry garlic until aromatic, about 1 minute. Add scallions and cook for 1 minute. Remove from heat. Spoon garlic and scallions over scallops.

Half fill a medium wok with water (steamer should not touch water) and bring to a boil. Working in batches, arrange scallops in a bamboo steamer, cover and place steamer over boiling water. Steam until scallops are tender, 7–10 minutes, adding more boiling water to wok when necessary. Lift steamer off wok and carefully remove scallops.

To make ginger and scallion sauce, place scallions in a small bowl and set aside. Heat oil in a small saucepan over medium heat and fry ginger and chili pepper until aromatic, about 1 minute. Remove from heat and stir in soy sauce and water. Bring to a boil and pour over scallions. Let stand for 2 minutes before serving with scallops.

Stir-fried squid with chili

Makes 4 small serves
4 cleaned squid tubes, about 12 oz (375 g) total
2 tablespoons vegetable oil
1 teaspoon Asian sesame oil
3 cloves garlic, finely chopped
1–2 small red chili peppers, seeded and finely chopped

Cut squid in half lengthwise, then cut into strips ¾ inch (2 cm) wide. Heat oils in a wok or frying pan over medium heat. Fry garlic and chili pepper until aromatic, about 1 minute. Add squid and stir-fry for 1 minute. Do not overcook or squid will become tough. Remove from heat and serve hot.

Clams with black bean sauce

Serves 6–8

1 lb (500 g) fresh clams in shells, shells cleaned

BLACK BEAN SAUCE

2 teaspoons vegetable oil

2 cloves garlic, finely chopped

2 teaspoons peeled and grated fresh ginger

2 teaspoons fermented black beans, rinsed and chopped

2 tablespoons soy sauce

⅓ cup (3 fl oz/90 ml) water

2 tablespoons oyster sauce

Place clams in a bamboo steamer and cover with lid. Half fill a medium wok with water (steamer should not touch water) and bring to a boil. Place steamer over boiling water and steam until clam shells open, 3–4 minutes (discard any clams that do not open). Lift steamer off wok and carefully remove clams.

To make black bean sauce, heat oil in a small saucepan over medium heat. Fry garlic and ginger until aromatic, about 1 minute. Add black beans, soy sauce, water and oyster sauce. Bring to a boil, reduce heat and simmer for 1 minute. Serve drizzled over clams.

Steamed pork ribs

Makes 8 small servings
1 lb (500 g) pork spare ribs, trimmed and cut into 3¼-inch (8-cm) lengths
(ask your butcher to prepare these for you)
1 tablespoon rice wine
1 teaspoon salt
2 teaspoons superfine (caster) sugar
1 teaspoon Asian sesame oil
4 cloves garlic, finely chopped
2 tablespoons fermented black beans, washed and chopped
½ teaspoon dry chili flakes
2 teaspoons cornstarch (cornflour)
½ red bell pepper (capsicum), seeded and finely shredded

Place ribs in a shallow dish. Combine rice wine, salt, sugar, sesame oil, garlic, black beans, chili flakes and cornstarch and mix well. Pour over ribs, cover and refrigerate for 2 hours.

Half fill a medium wok with water (steamer should not touch water) and bring to a boil. Working in batches, place ribs on a heatproof plate and put it into a bamboo steamer. Cover and place steamer over boiling water. Steam until ribs are tender, about 25 minutes, adding more boiling water to wok when necessary. Lift steamer off wok and carefully remove ribs. Garnish with shredded red bell pepper.

Barbecue pork, Chinese style

Makes 8 small servings
2 pork fillets, 12 oz (375 g) each
3 tablespoons hoisin sauce
3 tablespoons ground bean sauce
2 cloves garlic, crushed
¼ teaspoon Chinese five-spice powder
3 tablespoons soy sauce
pinch of Chinese red food coloring powder (optional)
1 tablespoon brown sugar

Place pork fillets in a shallow dish. Combine hoisin sauce, ground bean sauce, garlic, five-spice powder, soy sauce, red food coloring and brown sugar, and mix well. Pour over pork and toss until well coated in marinade. Cover and refrigerate overnight.

Drain pork and reserve marinade. Place pork on a wire rack over a baking dish. Bake at 350°F (180°C/Gas 4) for 30 minutes, basting with marinade and turning pork during cooking.

Remove from oven and allow to stand for 10 minutes before slicing. Serve hot or cold.

Chinese vegetables with oyster sauce

Serves 4

2 tablespoons oyster sauce

3 tablespoons chicken stock

2 teaspoons soy sauce

1 teaspoon Asian sesame oil

1 teaspoon cornstarch (cornflour) mixed with 1 tablespoon chicken stock

1 bunch garlic chives, tied into a bundle with string, or choy sum or bok choy, trimmed into 4-inch (10-cm) lengths and tied with string

In a small saucepan, combine oyster sauce, stock, soy sauce, sesame oil and cornstarch mixture. Bring to a boil over medium heat, stirring until sauce bubbles and thickens. Remove from heat.

Blanch garlic chives or Chinese vegetables in a saucepan of boiling water for 1 minute. Remove from pan with a slotted spoon, place on serving plate and remove string. Tie one of the chives around bundle, pour oyster sauce over it and serve.

Grilled mushrooms

Makes 4 small servings
13 oz (400 g) shiitake mushrooms, stems trimmed
2 tablespoons soy sauce
2 tablespoons mirin
1 tablespoon superfine (caster) sugar
1 tablespoon chopped chives
2 teaspoons black sesame seeds mixed with 1 teaspoon chopped chives

Place mushrooms in a shallow dish. Combine soy sauce, mirin, sugar and chives, and pour over mushrooms. Cover and marinate for 5 minutes. Drain mushrooms and reserve marinade.

Place mushrooms on a lightly oiled tray and cook under a preheated hot broiler (grill) until softened, about 3 minutes on each side. Brush with marinade during cooking. Arrange mushrooms in small bowls or plates, and sprinkle with black sesame seed and chive mixture. Serve hot.

Desserts

Chinese custard tarts

Makes 24
PASTRY
3 cups (12 oz/375 g) all-purpose (plain) flour
6 oz (180 g) lard
5 tablespoons hot water
FILLING
3 eggs
⅓ cup (2 oz/ 60 g) superfine (caster) sugar
1½ cups (12 fl oz/375 ml) milk
yellow food coloring (optional)

To make pastry, sift flour into a bowl. Using your fingertips, rub lard into flour, until mixture resembles coarse breadcrumbs. Add hot water and mix to form a firm dough. Turn dough out onto a floured work surface and knead until smooth. Roll out between 2 sheets of parchment (baking paper) to ⅛ inch (3 mm) thick. Using a 3-inch (8-cm) round cutter, cut dough into 24 rounds. Line greased tart (patty) pans with dough.

To make filling, beat eggs, sugar, milk and a few drops of food coloring (if using) together until smooth. Pour into prepared pastry. Bake at 425°F (220°C/Gas 7) for 10 minutes. Reduce oven temperature to 400°F (200°C/Gas 6) and bake until custard is set, 10–15 minutes. Remove from oven and allow to stand for 10 minutes before transferring to a wire rack to cool. Serve cold or chilled.

Sweet coconut bards

Makes 16 pieces

2½ cups (17½ oz/545 g) glutinous
    rice

2¼ cups (18 fl oz/560 ml) coconut
    milk

½ cup (3¼ oz/110 g) superfine
    (caster) sugar

TOPPING

1¼ cups (5 oz/150 g) unsweetened
    shredded (desiccated) coconut

¼ cup (2 fl oz/60 ml) coconut milk,
    warmed

3 oz (90 g) grated palm sugar
    or brown sugar

3 tablespoons water

Place rice in a large bowl, cover with cold water and let stand overnight. Line a large bamboo steamer with parchment (baking paper) and spread drained rice on top. Cover steamer.

Half fill a medium wok with water (steamer should not touch water) and bring to a boil. Place steamer over boiling water and steam until rice is tender, about 45 minutes, adding more boiling water to wok when necessary.

Place steamed rice into a medium, heavy-bottomed saucepan. Add coconut milk and sugar. Stir over low heat until the coconut milk has been absorbed, about 10 minutes. Evenly spread rice into a shallow baking pan about 7½ x 11 inches (19 x 28 cm) lined with parchment (baking paper). Refrigerate until firm, about 2 hours.

For topping, combine coconut and coconut milk. Place palm sugar and water in a small saucepan, stir over low heat until mixture thickens slightly, 3–4 minutes. Pour into coconut and milk mixture, stir until well combined. Allow to cool to room temperature. Spread topping over rice and refrigerate for 1 hour. Cut into small squares to serve.

Almond pudding

These tiny gelatic squares can be served with any fresh fruit.

Makes 16
2 cups (16 fl oz/500 ml) cold water
⅓ cup (2 oz/60 g) superfine (caster) sugar
5 teaspoons gelatin
⅔ cup (5 fl oz/160 ml) evaporated milk
½ teaspoon almond extract
mango slices for serving

Place water and sugar in a saucepan. Sprinkle gelatin over top. Bring mixture to a boil, stirring for 1 minute. Remove from heat. Add evaporated milk and almond extract, and mix well. Pour into an oiled pan about 7½ by 11 inches (18 by 28 cm). Refrigerate until firm, 2–3 hours. Cut into small squares and serve with slices of fresh mango.

Dipping Sauces

Sweet cilantro sauce

Makes 1 cup (8 fl oz/250 ml)
¼ cup (2 oz/60 g) superfine (caster) sugar
¾ cup (6 fl oz/180 ml) white vinegar
¼ cup (2 fl oz/60 ml) water
1 small red chili pepper, seeded and sliced
2 scallions (shallots/spring onions), sliced
1 tablespoon finely chopped fresh cilantro (coriander)
½ small cucumber, seeded and chopped

Place sugar, vinegar and water in a small saucepan, stir over low heat until sugar dissolves. Remove from heat and stir in chili pepper, scallions, cilantro and cucumber.

Ginger soy dipping sauce

Makes ⅔ cup (5 fl oz/150 ml)
3 teaspoons peeled and grated fresh ginger
½ cup (4 fl oz/125 ml) light soy sauce
2 tablespoons Thai sweet chili sauce

Combine ginger, soy sauce and chili sauce, and mix well.

Lime and cilantro dipping sauce

Makes ¼ cup (2 fl oz/60 ml)
2 tablespoons fish sauce
2 tablespoons white vinegar
2 tablespoons fresh lime juice
½ teaspoon superfine (caster) sugar
2 tablespoons finely chopped fresh cilantro (coriander)

Combine fish sauce, vinegar, lime juice, sugar and cilantro, and mix well.

Quick sweet-and-sour sauce

Makes 1½ cups (12 fl oz/375 ml)
1½ cups (12 fl oz/375 ml) pineapple
   juice
2 tablespoons tomato ketchup
2 teaspoons tomato paste (concentrate)
2 tablespoons superfine (caster) sugar
3 tablespoons white vinegar

Place all ingredients in a medium
saucepan and bring to a boil. Reduce
heat to low, simmer for 10 minutes,
stirring occasionally. Remove from
heat and allow to cool.

Easy plum sauce

Makes 1 cup (8 fl oz/250 ml)
5 tablespoons plum jam
½ cup (4 fl oz/125 ml) rice wine
   vinegar
1 small red chili pepper, seeded
   and thinly sliced

Place jam and vinegar in a small
saucepan. stir over medium heat until
jam melts, about 3 minutes. Remove
from heat and allow to cool. Just
before serving, stir chili into sauce.

Lime and fish sauce

Makes ½ cup (4 fl oz/125 ml)
½ cup (4 fl oz/125 ml) lime juice
2 teaspoons grated palm sugar
   or brown sugar
2 teaspoons fish sauce
1 teaspoon finely chopped scallion
   (shallot/spring onion)
1 teaspoon finely chopped, seeded
   red chili pepper
1 teaspoon peeled and grated
   fresh ginger

Place lime juice in a bowl. Add sugar
and stir until sugar dissolves. Add
fish sauce, scallion, chili pepper and
ginger, and mix well.

Chili sauce

Makes ½ cup (4 fl oz/125 ml)
2 teaspoons sambal oelek
½ cup (4 fl oz/125 ml) rice wine
1 teaspoon superfine (caster) sugar
1 tablespoon finely chopped scallions
   (shallots/spring onions)

Combine sambal oelek, rice wine,
sugar and scallions, and mix well.

Glossary

BEAN CURD Also known as tofu, bean curd is made from soaked yellow soybeans ground into a puree and cooked in water. A coagulant is added to the resultant soy milk, the whey is drained off and the curds are lightly pressed. Fresh bean curd is available in soft or firm varieties. Once open, store in a bowl of water in the refrigerator. Bean curd is sold in the refrigerated section of Asian markets.

BEAN SPROUTS Sprouting green mung beans, sold fresh or canned. Fresh sprouts tend to have a crisper texture and a more delicate flavor. Store in refrigerator for up to 3 days.

BLACK BEANS These salted and fermented soybeans are available in cans or packets from Asian markets. They should be rinsed before use as they can be very salty. Store unused black beans in a covered container in refrigerator.

CHINESE BARBECUE PORK Also known as cha siu. Boneless pork that has been marinated in Chinese five-spice powder and soy sauce, and then roasted. Sold in slices or strips in Chinese markets. Stores for up to 2 days in refrigerator.

CHINESE ROAST DUCK Sold freshly roasted in Chinese markets and delicious in stir-fries or on its own. Use 1–2 days after purchase. Substitute roast chicken if unavailable.

CILANTRO Pungent, fragrant leaves from the coriander plant, resembling parsley and also called Chinese parsley and coriander. Leaves and roots are used widely in Southeast Asian cuisine.

COCONUT MILK Rich liquid extracted from shredded coconut that has been steeped in water. It is used in sweet and savory Asian dishes. Coconut milk is available canned.

FISH SAUCE Pungent sauce of salted fermented fish and other seasonings. Products vary in intensity depending on the country of origin. Fish sauce from Thailand, called nam pla, is a commonly available variety.

FIVE-SPICE POWDER This fragrant blend of spices is used extensively in Chinese cooking. It contains star anise, Sichuan peppercorns, fennel, cloves and cinnamon. Use sparingly.

GINGER Thick, rootlike rhizome of the ginger plant, with a sharp, pungent flavor. Once the thin, tan skin is peeled from fresh ginger, the flesh is grated or sliced. Store fresh ginger in refrigerator for up to 3 days.

GOW GEE PRESS A special (usually plastic) utensil for making gow gee (semicircular dumplings). Presses are sold in Asian markets.

GROUND BEAN SAUCE A commercial sauce made from soybeans, sugar, salt, sesame oil and flour and sold in Asian markets.

LOTUS NUT PASTE Traditionally used as the filling for Chinese moon cakes, lotus nut paste is made from the seeds of the lotus plant. It is sold in cans in Asian markets.

MIRIN Sweet alcoholic wine made from rice. Store in a cool, dark place after opening. Sweet sherry can be substituted.

PALM SUGAR Dense, heavy, dark cakes made from the sap of palm trees and sold in Asian markets. Shave with a sharp knife or grate before using. Substitute brown sugar if unavailable.

RED BEAN PASTE Boiled, mashed and sweetened azuki beans, sold in cans in Asian markets.

OYSTER SAUCE Thick, dark brown Chinese sauce made from fermented dried oysters and soy sauce, and used to impart an intense or mild briny flavor to stir-fries and other dishes. Store in refrigerator after opening.

SAMBAL OELEK Spicy Indonesian paste consisting of ground chili peppers combined with salt and occasionally vinegar. It can be used as a substitute for fresh chili peppers.

SOY SAUCE Salty sauce made from fermented soybeans and usually wheat, used as an ingredient and as a table condiment. Dark soy sauce is thicker and often less salty than light soy sauce. Low-sodium products are also available.

THAI SWEET CHILI SAUCE Mild, sweet chili sauce used as a flavoring and as a dipping sauce. Store in refrigerator after opening.

Index

Cover picture: Cockscomb dumplings, see page 26
Pictured on page 2: Salmon money bags, see page 25
Pictured on page 4: Steamed spinach and ginger dumplings, see page 32

A LANSDOWNE BOOK

Published by Apple Press
Sheridan House
4th Floor
112-116 Western Road
Hove
East Sussex BN3 1DD UK

Copyright © 2002 text, photography and design: Lansdowne Publishing Pty Ltd

Created and produced by Lansdowne Publishing
Text: Vicki Liley
Photographer: Louise Lister
Stylist: Vicki Liley
Designer: Avril Makula
Editor: Joanne Holliman
Production Manager: Sally Stokes
Project Coordinator: Kate Merrifield

ISBN 1 84092 429 2

Set in Trade Gothic, Journal Text, Gill Sans and Neuropol on QuarkXPress
Printed in Singapore by Kyodo Printing Pte Ltd